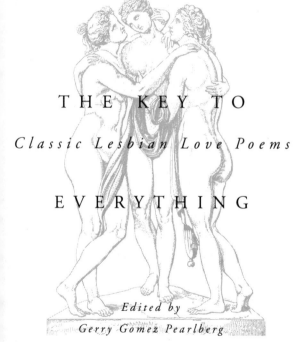

THE KEY TO

Classic Lesbian Love Poems

EVERYTHING

Edited by
Gerry Gomez Pearlberg

A Stonewall Inn Book
St. Martin's Press / New York

Design by Jaye Zimet

Library of Congress Cataloging-in-Publication Data

The key to everything: classic lesbian love poems / [compiled by] Gerry
   Gomez Pearlberg.
       p.   cm.
   ISBN 0-312-11842-2
   1. Love poetry.   2. Lesbians' writings.   I. Pearlberg, Gerry.
PN6110.L6K49   1995
808.81'9354—dc20   94-36025
                                                                CIP

First Edition: February 1995

10   9   8   7   6   5   4   3   2   1

The editor and the publisher are grateful for permission to reprint the copy-righted poems in this anthology. Permissions appear on pages 84–87, which constitute a continuation of this copyright page.

Acknowledgments

My deepest appreciation goes out to Joan Larkin for the practical assistance, moral support, and kind advice she offered me at various points in the process of working on this book. I am also grateful to Joan Nestle for her sleuthing skills and her generous encouragement in this and so much else.

I would also like to thank Michele Karlsberg for recommending me for this project; Deb Edel and the Lesbian Herstory Archives for being a gold mine of information; Linda L. Nelson for the helpful faxes; Degania Golove of the June Mazer Collection for her assistance in locating the estate of Elsa Gidlow; and Stephanie Gilman for advising me on the Rossetti question.

One of the great joys of working on this book was having the opportunity to interact with so many poets whose work I admire. I thank them for their powerful words, and for making this experience such an enriching one.

LOVE POEM

Speak earth and bless me
with what is richest
make sky flow honey out of my hips
rigid as mountains
spread over a valley
carved out by the mouth of rain.

And I knew when I entered her   I was
high wind in her forest's hollow
fingers whispering sound
honey flowed   from the split cup
impaled on a lance of tongues
on the tips of her breasts   on her navel
and my breath   howling into her entrances
through lungs of pain.

Greedy as herring-gulls
or a child
I swing out   over the earth
over and over   again.

LOOKING AT EACH OTHER

Yes, we were looking at each other
Yes, we knew each other very well
Yes, we had made love with each other many times
Yes, we had heard music together
Yes, we had gone to the sea together
Yes, we had cooked and eaten together
Yes, we had laughed often day and night
Yes, we fought violence and knew violence
Yes, we hated the inner and outer oppression
Yes, that day we were looking at each other
Yes, we saw the sunlight pouring down
Yes, the corner of the table was between us
Yes, bread and flowers were on the table
Yes, our eyes saw each other's eyes
Yes, our mouths saw each other's mouth
Yes, our breasts saw each other's breasts
Yes, our bodies entire saw each other
Yes, it was beginning in each
Yes, it threw waves across our lives
Yes, the pulses were becoming very strong
Yes, the beating became very delicate
Yes, the calling   the arousal
Yes, the arriving   the coming
Yes, there it was for both entire
Yes, we were looking at each other

WHEN I CALL YOUR NAME

July is over, four hot weeks
Of August, two long weeks in September,
And then I'll be in your bedroom, in your bed,
Nibbling your pink earlobe.

Even in the city, our day will be
Luscious, your hair black and twining
In my hands like the wild muscadine grape.
Scuppernong brown, your nipples will be full
Against my mouth. We will look through
Barred windows at night for the harvest moon.
Equinox soon will diminish the light.
Tell me, love, how to speed time now,
How to slow it then, when I call your name.

MADONNA OF THE
EVENING FLOWERS

All day long I have been working,
Now I am tired.
I call: "Where are you?"
But there is only the oak-tree rustling in the wind.
The house is very quiet,
The sun shines in on your books,
On your scissors and thimble just put down,
But you are not there.
Suddenly I am lonely:
Where are you?
I go about searching.

Then I see you,
Standing under a spire of pale blue larkspur,
With a basket of roses on your arm.
You are cool, like silver,
And you smile.
I think the Canterbury bells are playing little tunes.

You tell me that the peonies need spraying,
That the columbines have overrun all bounds,
That the pyrus japonica should be cut back and
        rounded.
You tell me these things.

But I look at you, heart of silver,
White heart-flame of polished silver,
Burning beneath the blue steeples of the larkspur,
And I long to kneel instantly at your feet,
While all about us peal the loud, sweet *Te Deums*
    of the Canterbury bells.

FOUR BEGINNINGS
FOR KYRA

1. You raise
    your face from mine, parting
    my breath like water, hair falling
    away in its own wind, and your eyes—
    green in the light like honey—surfacing
    on my body, awed
    with desire, speechless, this common dream.

2. You bore your marriage like a misconceived
    animal, and have the scars, the pale
    ridged tissue round front and back
    for proof.   For proof.   Tonight

    we cross into each other's language.   I take your
         hand
    hesitant still with regret
    into that milky landscape, where braille
    is a tongue for lovers, where tongue,
    fingers, lips
    share a lidless eye.

3. I was surprised myself—the image of the lithe
   hermaphroditic lover a staple of
   every fantasy, bought, borrowed, or mine.   We
       never did
   mention the word, unqualified: I love:
   your hair, I love: your feet, toes, tender nibbles,
       I love:

   I love.   You are the memory
   of each desire that ran, dead-end, into a mind
   programmed to misconstrue it.   A mind
       inventing
   neurosis, anxiety, phobia, a mind expertly
       camouflaged
   from the thought of love
   for a woman, its native
   love.

4. I in my narrow body, spellbound
   against your flesh.

FROM TWENTY-ONE
LOVE POEMS

X

Your dog, tranquil and innocent, dozes through
our cries, our murmured dawn conspiracies
our telephone calls. She knows—what can she know?
If in my human arrogance I claim to read
her eyes, I find there only my own animal thoughts:
that creatures must find each other for bodily
        comfort,
that voices of the psyche drive through the flesh
further than the dense brain could have foretold,
that the planetary nights are growing cold for those
on the same journey who want to touch
one creature-traveler clear to the end;
that without tenderness, we are in hell.

OF ALTHEA AND FLAXIE

In 1943 Althea was a welder
very dark
very butch
and very proud
loved to cook, sew, and drive a car
and did not care who knew she kept company
     with a woman
who met her every day after work
in a tight dress and high heels
light-skinned and high-cheekboned
who loved to shoot, fish, play poker
and did not give a damn who knew her 'man'
     was a woman.

Althea was gay and strong in 1945
and could sing a good song
from underneath her welder's mask
and did not care who heard her sing her song
     to a woman.

Flaxie was careful and faithful
mindful of her Southern upbringing
watchful of her tutored grace
long as they treated her like a lady

she did not give a damn who called her
    a 'bulldagger.'

In 1950 Althea wore suits and ties
Flaxie's favorite colors were pink and blue
People openly challenged their flamboyance
but neither cared a fig who thought them 'queer'
    or 'funny.'

When the girls bragged over break of their
    sundry loves,
Flaxie blithely told them her old lady Althea took
    her dancing
every weekend
and did not give a damn who knew she clung
    to a woman.

When the boys on her shift complained of their wives,
Althea boasted of how smart her 'stuff' Flaxie was
and did not care who knew she loved the mind of a
    woman.

In 1955 when Flaxie got pregnant
and Althea lost her job

Flaxie got herself on relief
and did not care how many caseworkers
threatened midnite raids.

Althea was set up and went to jail
for writing numbers in 1958.
Flaxie visited her every week with gifts
and hungered openly for her thru the bars
and did not give a damn who knew she waited
     for a woman.

When her mother died in 1965 in New Orleans
Flaxie demanded that Althea walk beside her in the
     funeral procession
and did not care how many aunts and uncles knew
     she slept with a woman.

When she died in 1970
Flaxie fought Althea's proper family not to have her
     laid out in lace
and dressed the body herself
and did not care who knew she'd made her way with
     a woman.

THE WESTERN UNION LADY

She had a funny look on her face
the western union lady
she didn't know
that I had to be with you
right then
but the best I could do was a telegram

she didn't know
that I was used to seeing four legs
when I looked down at the sidewalk
and my own two legs were just not enough

she didn't know
that the space in the air
where your hand was supposed to be
was so cold and empty
that the brittle traffic noise
was supposed to be filtered by your soft voice

the best I could do was a telegram
I took the order form and wrote
"I want to touch your skin
and lick your stomach"

the western union lady
had a funny look on her face
but she said it would only take a day

What did she sound like?
the western union lady in Ohio
when she said to you over the phone
"I want to lick your stomach"

Wild Nights—Wild Nights!
Were I with thee
Wild Nights should be
Our luxury!

Futile—the Winds—
To a Heart in port—
Done with the Compass—
Done with the Chart!

Rowing in Eden—
Ah, the Sea!
Might I but moor—Tonight—
In Thee!

AT NIGHT

I want to hold you
in a motel room
with the sunshine stripe
of venetian blinds
across your back.
Or I want the dream of that.

My large breasts press down,
you drink my sweat,
I push inside
hoping for endless night,
mining for release.

Against the white sheet
you are young supple limbs
and dark thought.
I fear your newness,
my need to make you old.
All my words prelude
to this command of your body
locked in half secret by solid bands
of afternoon and evening
painted across the room.

Your hand is firm
in the rope of my hair.
The highway circles outside
and day blinks by.
You bend over me
and the shadow is not cool.
I want to press my mouth
to your sighs
sucking in your insistent movement.
Or I want the dream of that.

NEW BODY

There's a sort of eternity
when we're in bed together
whether silently you awaken
me with the flat of your hand
or sleep breathing with a small scratch
in your throat, or quietly attach
a bird to the sky I dream
as a way in to my body—

Now you have made me excited
to accept heaven as an idea
inside us, perpetual
waters, because you let yourself
fall from a sky you invented
to a sea I vaulted
when it was small rain
accumulating—My heart drained

there and fills now in time
to sketch in the entire
desert landscape we remember
as an ocean port,
that part of me accepting
your trust, a deep

voluptuous thrust into my hours,
that has no earthly power

but lives believing you were made for me
to give in to completely,
every entry into you the lip
of water that is in itself scant hope
broken into like sleep
by kisses—Policed in the desert
by a shooting star, we are the subversive
love scratched out of sky, o my visitor.

CONSTANCY

You're jealous if I kiss this girl and that,
You think I should be constant to one mouth?
Little you know of my too quenchless drouth:
My sister, I keep faith with love, not lovers.

Life laid a flaming finger on my heart,
Gave me an electric golden thread,
Pointed to a pile of beads and said:
Link me one more glorious than the rest.

Love's the thread, my sister, you a bead,
An ivory one, you are so delicate.
Those first burned ash-grey—far too passionate.
Further on the colors mount and sing.

When the last bead's painted with the last design
And slipped upon the thread, I'll tie it: so;
Then smiling quietly I'll turn and go
While vain Life boasts her latest ornament.

Didn't Sappho say her guts clutched up like this?
Before a face suddenly numinous,
her eyes watered, knees melted. Did she lactate
again, milk brought down by a girl's kiss?
It's documented torrents are unloosed
by such events as recently produced
not the wish, but the need, to consume, in us,
one pint of Maalox, one of Kaopectate.
My eyes and groin are permanently swollen,
I'm alternatingly brilliant and witless
—and sleepless: bed is just a swamp to roll in.
Although I'd cream my jeans touching your breast,
sweetheart, it isn't lust; it's all the rest
of what I want with you that scares me shitless.

I LIKE A WOMAN WHO PACKS

not because she wants to be a man because she knows
I want a butch
who can loop my wrist with leather, whisper
    Stay right here
I have something I need to do to you
who can smile wide when I ask her to dance
because I've noticed the bulge in her pants
Tells me to come back for a slow number
because she doesn't do fast
I like a woman who'll make me beg her for it
Ride me till I forget my name, the date
the president, prime minister & every head of state
I like to sashay down the street a bit
with her watching my legs & breasts & ass
while I watch her hands & mouth
& the neighbors gasp
I like a woman who can make me over
into whatever she wants
as long as she wants
wet & hungry to my heart
I like it when she grabs my hair
says   *Don't move until I tell you*
I like a woman who packs
stands behind me in a crowded room leaning into
    my back

whispers in my ear
Hey you wanna give it up to me?
I like her tall or short   heavy or slim
walking or riding a chair   brown or pink   old or
       young
I like a woman who can take me under
when she takes me over
then let me suck her, get in trouble, snap her gloves
I like a woman who wants to be
the best fuck I've ever had
I like a woman who snacks

FOR WILLYCE

When i make love to you
   i try
      with each stroke of my tongue
         to say   i love you
         to tease   i love you
         to hammer   i love you
         to melt   i love you

   & your sounds drift down
      oh god!
         oh jesus!
     and i think—
here it is, some dude's
getting credit for what
      a woman
      has done,
         again.

BLACK SLIP

She told me she had always fantasized
about a woman in a black slip.
It had to do with Elizabeth Taylor
in "Butterfield Eight."

She came to my house with a huge box
gift-wrapped with gigantic ribbons.
Inside, a black slip.
Slinky, with lace across the bodice.
She told me how she was embarrassed
in the department store,
a woman in men's pants
buying a black slip clearly not intended for herself,
and about the gay men in line behind her,
sharing the joke.

She asked me to try it on.
I took it into the bathroom, slipped it over my head.
I stared at myself for a long time
before I came out of the bathroom
walked over to her
lying on the bed.

That was the first time. It got easier.
The black slip was joined by a blue slip

then a red one
then a long lavender negligee, the back slit to there.

I wore them to bed.
In the morning she would smile and say
how much she loved waking up next to a woman in
    a slip.
The black slip remained our favorite.
We always made love when I wore the black slip.

Once I showed up at her door late at night
wearing a long coat
with only the black slip underneath.

One night I cooked dinner at her apartment
wearing nothing but the black slip
and red suede high heels.

It was always the first thing to pack when we went
    on vacation.

And she used to make me promise
that if we ever broke up
I'd never wear that slip for anyone else.

I don't know where it is now.

Stripped of that private skin
when we broke up
I never went back to claim it.

I think she must have
packed it
given it
thrown it
away.

On bad days I imagine her
sliding it over the head of some new love
whispering about Elizabeth Taylor
and waking up to a woman in a slip.

Or perhaps
it's still there
draped on the back of the door.

A sinuous shadow.

A moan in the dark.

PORN POEMS

Her tongue & her
heart were
throbbing
in the holster
of her pussy.

INSIDE YOUR SILENT ARMS

Dreams bite my ears, I pretend it is you
whispering, and nibbling, and holding me
and I can twist, and I can turn, and you
can not let go, but the dreams still bite me.
I hear you whispering it is okay,
we will be together for the rest of
the night, oh, and the rest of the day, and
the rest of the world won't at all matter.
I need only feel your breath upon me,
in, around my ear, and dream of the rest . . .
I want to forget all the empty past,
oh, nights when I dreamt hollow, woke screaming,
times too many dreams collided in me
and the television would not turn off.

I OFFER YOU PERSIMMONS

this persimmon
is my mouth   offered like tea leaves
to be read   or tarot cards   lined palms
pure   immutable longing   just beneath the skin
traces of desire like fingerprints   blood stains
DNA   I want to make this offering to you
pure   unblemished fruit   arching   swollen
with silent prayer   soundless adoration
silent golden fruit   sliced to take
between your lips   that
hallowed place
i've yet to
find

A VALENTINE

What shall I send my sweet today,
  When all the woods attune in love?
  And I would show the lark and dove,
That I can love as well as they.

I'll send a locket full of hair,—
  But no, for it might chance to lie
  Too near her heart, and I should die
Of love's sweet envy to be there.

A violet is sweet to give,—
  Ah, stay! she'd touch it with her lips,
  And, after such complete eclipse,
How could my soul consent to live?

I'll send a kiss, for that would be
  The quickest sent, the lightest borne,
  And well I know tomorrow morn
She'll send it back again to me.

Go, happy winds; ah, do not stay,
  Enamoured of my lady's cheek,
  But hasten home, and I'll bespeak
Your services another day!

FROM GOBLIN MARKET

'LAURA AND LIZZIE ASLEEP'

Golden head by golden head,
Like two pigeons in one nest
Folded in each other's wings,
They lay down in their curtained bed:
Like two blossoms on one stem,
Like two flakes of new-fall'n snow,
Like two wands of ivory
Tipped with gold for awful kings.
Moon and stars gazed in at them,
Wind sang to them lullaby,
Lumbering owls forbore to fly,
Not a bat flapped to and fro
Round their nest:
Cheek to cheek and breast to breast
Locked together in one nest.

I have had not one word from her

Frankly I wish I were dead.
When she left, she wept

a great deal; she said to
me, "This parting must be
endured, Sappho. I go unwillingly."

I said, "Go, and be happy
but remember (you know
well) whom you leave shackled by love

"If you forget me, think
of our gifts to Aphrodite
and all the loveliness that we shared

"all the violet tiaras,
braided rosebuds, dill and
crocus twined around your young neck

"myrrh poured on your head
and on soft mats girls with
all that they most wished for beside them

"while no voices chanted
choruses without ours,
no woodlot bloomed in spring without song . . ."

TRANSLATED BY MARY BARNARD

POEM FOR PAT

I wanted you to hear that song
she told me
so I listened and listened
trying to understand why
even admitting it was lovely
heart provoking
I still wondered
it took me clean through winter
and past full-bodied trees
into another snow.
Well I'll be damned, here comes your ghost again—

It happened to be on the day
we found each other again she said
and we were shivering at what we contemplated
locked together on the sandstone mesa at star
    rock
we were looking everywhere, she said
diné country spread at our feet
we could hear the coydogs howling far off
and watch the chindi- -dust devils
whirl their plans on the floor below
watch for rain.
Our breath comes out white clouds,
mingles and hangs in the air

there were cedars twisted near where we sat.
It was spring.

Today the sun flows softly through my window
and I'm listening to the song,
thinking of her again on that mesa
wondering what mystery materialized out of that
        wind
and if it rained.

My divine Lysis:
do forgive my daring,
if so I address you,
unworthy though I am to be known as yours.

   I cannot think it bold
to call you so, well knowing
you've ample thunderbolts
to shatter any overweening of mine.

   It's the tongue that misspeaks
when what is called dominion—
I mean, the master's rule—
is made to seem possession by the slave.

   The vassal says: my king;
my prison, the convict says;
and any humble slave
will call the master his without offense.

   Thus, when I call you mine,
it's not that I expect
you'll be considered such—
only that I hope I may be yours.

   I saw you—need more be said?
To broadcast a fire,
telling the cause suffices—
no need to apportion blame for the effect.

Seeing you so exalted
does not prevent my daring;
no god is ever secure
against the lofty flight of human thought.
    There are women more deserving,
yet in distance from heaven
the humblest of valleys
seems no farther than the highest peak.
    In sum, I must admit
to the crime of adoring you;
should you wish to punish me,
the very punishment will be reward.

TRANSLATED BY ALAN S. TRUEBLOOD

THE KEY TO EVERYTHING

Is there anything I can do
or has everything been done
or do
you prefer someone else to do
it or don't
you trust me to do
it right or is it hopeless and no one can do
a thing or do
you suppose I don't
really want to do
it and am just saying that or don't
you hear me at all or what?

You're
waiting for
the right person the doctor or
the nurse the father or
the mother or
the person with the name you keep
mumbling in your sleep
that no one ever heard of there's no one
named that really
except yourself maybe

If I knew what your name was I'd
prove it's your
own name spelled backwards or
twisted in some way the one you
keep mumbling but you
won't tell me your
name or
don't you know it
yourself that's it
of course you've
forgotten or
never quite knew it or
weren't willing to believe it

Then there *is* something I
can do I
can find your name for you
that's the key to everything once you'd
repeat it clearly you'd
come awake you'd
get up and walk knowing where you're
going where you
came from

And you'd
love me
after that or would you
hate me?
no once you'd
get there you'd
remember and love me
of course I'd
be gone by then I'd
be far away

Irena Klepfisz

PERIODS OF STRESS

it is unwise during periods of stress
or change to formulate new theories.
case in point: when about to begin
a new love affair   without having ended
the previous one   do not maintain
that more freedom is required for the full expression
of individual personality   or that various
life styles are possible   and all kinds of interesting
situations   still need to be explored.

try instead: i am tired   tired
of the nearness   this small apartment
of the watering can and level of the window
shade.   i prefer to drift toward more spacious rooms
towards intimate restaurants and dimly lit unfamiliar
beds   new love techniques.   but
do not throw me out.   i am too
frightened to venture out alone.
let me stay till i'm secure again
somewhere else   and then leave me alone.

JEALOUSY

From five hundred miles away
jealousy can hear
the crumpling of a pillow
beneath two heads.

CHANGING WHAT WE MEAN

Turning your back, you button your blouse.
    That's new.
You redirect the conversation. A man
has entered it. Your therapist has given you
permission to discuss this with me, the word
you've been looking for in desire.
You can now say "heterosexual" with me. We mean

different things when we say it. I mean
the life I left behind forever. For you, it's a new
beginning, a stab at being normal again, a desire
to enter the world with a man
instead of a woman, and of course, there's the word
you won't claim for yourself anymore, you

who have children to think of, you
who have put me in line behind them and mean
to keep the order clear. It's really my word
against yours anymore in this new
language, in this battle over how a man
is about to enter this closed room of desire

we've gingerly exchanged keys to, and desire
isn't what's at issue anyway, you
say to me. Instead I learn a man

can protect you in a way a woman only means
to but never can, and this world is too new
when there's real life out there, word

after word for how normal looks, each word
cutting like scissors a profile of desire—
a man facing a woman, nothing particularly new
or interesting to me. I've wanted only to face you
and the world simultaneously, say what I mean
with my body, my choice to not be a man,

to be a woman with you, forget the man's
part or how his body is the word
for what touch can contain, what love means.
If this were only about desire,
you say, I'd still desire you.
But it isn't passion we're defining, new

consequences emerge when a man and desire
are part of the words we hurl, you
changing how you mean loving—this terrible,
        final news.

Janice Gould

A MARRIED WOMAN

One day you agreed to meet me
in my cold house on the hill.
You came early.
It was Saturday, raining.
I'd waited for you for days, weeks.
The evening before your visit
I'd set the table with a white cloth
and placed two purple iris
in a glass vase.
You came with your photographs and stories—
and then we made love
in my wide bed.

Outside, redwood trees scratched at the window
and rain came down
from thick rolling clouds.
We drank wine and ate bread,
we kissed and lay sleeping,
our mouths nearly touching.
Hours later, our lovemaking over,
I was restless, hungry.
I kissed the back of your neck,
stroked your thighs.
The rain was still falling.

Let's go, I said, *where there are horses.*
I was trembling with desire,
not sure how to bridge the distance.
Off we drove, slightly drunk,
with our bag of apples.

The horses were in an open field,
out in the green hills:
bay, chestnut, pinto, gray.
Come feed them, I said,
I'll show you how.

But you laughed
and wouldn't stand with me by the fence
where the horses stamped
and tossed their heads,
smelling the apples,
baring their teeth at one another
ready to nip and bite.
You were dismayed by their size,
their slobbering muzzles
and jealous natures,
the hot curious energy which brought them
to the fence and my outstretched hand.

Later you confided your fear of animals
as you lay in my arms
in the front seat of my car.
It was late and we were down
by the brown churning river.
The clouds had descended.
I thought about a fear of animals,
and then my mind went quiet.
I watched the rain batter the windshield.

A FAREWELL

For a while I shall still be leaving,
Looking back at you as you slip away
Into the magic islands of the mind.
But for a while now all alive, believing
That in a single poignant hour
We did say all that we could ever say
In a great flowing out of radiant power.
It was like seeing and then going blind.

After a while we shall be cut in two
Between real islands where you live
And a far shore where I'll no longer keep
The haunting image of your eyes, and you,
As pupils widen, widen to deep black
And I am able neither to love or grieve
Between fulfillment and heartbreak.
The time will come when I can go to sleep.

But for a while still, centered at last,
Contemplate a brief amazing union,
Then watch you leave and then let you go.
I must not go back to the murderous past
Nor force a passage through to some safe landing,
But float upon this moment of communion
Entranced, astonished by pure understanding—
Passionate love dissolved like summer snow.

LETTER IN LATE JULY

for M.

Dearest, I have resisted these, my first lines
in more than a year, waiting for you to pass
like a mood or a winter, but you persist—
a landscape. It's green,

that limpid pre-dusk hesitation at the
swell of New England summer, and I'm bereft.
The surge of comfort has thinned to a whisper:
I'm on my own

to ride the surprises: tears fast as fresh
blood: poems I wrote you two years ago appear
in the mail cold and published: I have no
address for you, or

phone. A horse, solitary, walks from a barn
against a sky white with near-night. A fawn
picks her way across a darkening road, pulls you
up out of me. You'd

be surprised, wouldn't you, to hear that tonight
I wept with frustration at no message from
a man I keep dreaming of: I'd leave women,
so eager am I

not to remind my heart of you. My roses
throb clear colors as night falls; a bird call cuts
the warm silence like a quick ax. Rebecca
looked me in the eye

today. You've done it, she said; you've got yourself
back. I nodded to her, post office tears still
blearing, contact lenses salt-fogged. Whatever
I might say is as

high school quaint as sobs at a mute answering
box. I quiz myself as if an answer could
alter my feelings as deftly as touching
a key reconciles

green words on a black screen. But nothing merges
painlessly enough with my memory. I
could cook a lambchop or murder mosquitoes.
I could go out or

hang out my towels. Set phrases rise to soothe me—
This too shall pass—and do, as does the sound of
the brook, of summer traffic on the road. White
mullions edge black glass;

it's night. *Broken hearts are nothing new.* It's past
three months. When I dream you, it's a haze, colors
that seem familiar. When it rains, I can hear
your voice say *listen.*

Ruth L. Schwartz

THE OFFERING

for Gladys

I am trying in your language
to explain the force beyond our knowing—
*"La fuerza que hace volver
las cosas a la tierra,"* I say, defining gravity,
after the bad news from the hospital,
and still, when I touch you anywhere,
lay even a lone finger on your arm, we turn translucent

with desire—like the blue-hazed eye of any
newborn, or the jeweled snake as it prepares
    to shed,
and though it cannot stop your crying, nor my leaving,
nor the dying of your brother, nor the virus blooming
    in his cells,

each time we touch again, the conversation of our
    skin resumes
exactly where we left it last.
We are, we are, our bodies say,
my arms a nest you fill completely,
your large, mortal fingers bringing me
as if orgasm were a place, unimaginably beautiful,

and surrounded by impassable cliffs.
Into this canyon of astonishment, we plunge,
racing the disappearing light—
no, not the light itself, but its disappearance,
as the body's long tongue leans to catch
each falling offering

WHITE BALLOON

"To love something you know
will die is holy."

Kaddish, AIDS Memorial,
New York, 1987

The air is gravid with life,
the cloudless sky swells
with souls, ascending.

I'm in charge of one young soul
tied to my wrist
with a string that won't break.

St. Veronica's, the end of June:
You weep beside me, hold
a candle steadily near the flame.

Earlier we were two ladies
shopping on Broadway. I recall
your wire of a body,

the delicate arc of ribs
and small breast above—this
as you quick-changed

in search of something radical,
feminine. Your terror of pink
amused me. You said:

Don't tell anyone
of this sudden reversal. I said:
I will, but I'll change your name.

Linda, it's the letting go
that terrifies: the night air
alive with rising ghosts,

the cries of strong men
grieving in each other's arms,
the ease with which we love.

THRUWAY

There is no order
here. I scrub floors and wipe
fur from the white metal range thinking

I will leave this place and then
not. I reach for your face,
waist. How we love people

in pieces. Here is your gray-green
tattoo inscribing the pale silk
above your breast, here your full

throated rendition of country
western melodramas as we
rattle down the thruway. Orchards race

up hillsides to toss globes
at the sun. My feet guide yours
among dancing worlds

always knowing where to step
next yet tearing my flesh as I
cross river and ridge in opposite

directions. We spin a thick
glass and its force makes us
hot and huge. We leave the smell

of hair burning behind us.

Love rode 1500 miles on a grey
hound bus & climbed in my window
one night to surprise
both of us.
the pleasure of that sleepy
shock has lasted a decade
now or more because she is
always still doing it and I am
always still pleased. I do indeed like
aggressive women
who come half a continent
just for me; I am not saying that patience
is virtuous, Love
like anybody else, comes to those who
wait actively
and leave their windows open.

FROM BEFORE THE FLOWERS
OF FRIENDSHIP FADED
FRIENDSHIP FADED

XXIX

I love my love with a v
Because it is like that
I love myself with a b
Because I am beside that
A king.
I love my love with an a
Because she is a queen
I love my love and a a is the best of then
Think well and be a king,
Think more and think again
I love my love with a dress and a hat
I love my love and not with this or with that
I love my love with a y because she is my bride
I love her with a d because she is my love beside
Thank you for being there
Nobody has to care
Thank you for being here
Because you are not there.
    And with and without me which is and without
        she she can be

late and then and how and all around we think and
found that it is
time to cry she and I.

FROM AUTUMN SEQUENCE

XIII

Next to the white window
half in the white light,
what can I say now, love love, cherish me?
Twin our mouths,
a perfect semblance?
Who touches stained glass holds one blue forearm,
one red elbow, yellow shoulder;
stay away, that vicious capacity shows itself
between the comic gestures; no perfume, no washing:
each morning two foam pillows mimic the texture,
the bedspread offers buds to play with middle fingers,
the language pours a storm against the stripped
      branches
lifting the sheet from the floor,
setting an imagined picture against the lamp base.
I stretch myself over each blue mountain.
A rainbow, one section, hung from a string that day.
One cotton bag hung from the low promising cloud
sways while I count each equation:
your smile where the scarring snips the wound free,
more open than any moon, any dark ring, crescent,
      visible, invisible,
oh love:
let me.

Gerry Gomez Pearlberg

TIDE POOL VALENTINE

O you of slicked-back mermaid hair
and soapstone skin tattooed
with fish sticks and fish bones,
you're spiked stalactite hanging low
in the salt-caked cave of my desire,
dangerously close to scraping bottom.

The arthritic ache of these my hands
which long to touch your trickled pool
to touch you there
and press their fingers to your cheek
and rub their knuckles in your briny stream
of iridescent weeds as dark as knives,
like blind cave fish blanched pink
by lack of light.

Submerge, submerge
your lips and breasts and nipple clips,
your barnacles in rocky silver slits,
the hot Cousteau of your lips frenching mine
like baby squid in soft curd cones.

Submerge, submerge
and keyhole limpet me   yes
bore your bright tangelo bones
through my crab heart
of soft-shelled stone.

FROM HARD AGAINST THE SOUL

I

this is you girl, this cut of road up
to blanchicheuse, this every turn a piece
of blue and earth carrying on, beating, rock and
ocean this wearing away, smoothing the insides
pearl of shell and coral

this is you girl, this is you all sides of me
hill road and dip through the coconut at manzanilla
this sea breeze shaped forest of sand and lanky palm
this wanting to fall, hanging, greening
quenching the road

this is you girl, even though you never see it
the drop before timberline, that daub of black shine
sea on bush smoke land, that pulse of the heart
that stretches up to maracas, la fillete bay never know
you but you make it wash up from the rocks

this is you girl, that bit of lagoon, alligator
long abandoned, this stone of my youngness
hesitating to walk right, turning to Schoener's road
turning to duenne and spirit, to the sea wall and sea
breaking hard against things, turning to burning reason

this is you girl, this is the poem no woman
ever write for a woman because she 'fraid to touch
this river boiling like a woman in she sleep
that smell of fresh thighs and warm sweat
sheets of her like the mitan rolling into the atlantic

this is you girl, something never waning or forgetting
something hard against the soul
this is where you make sense, that the sight becomes
tender, the night air human, the dull silence full
chattering, volcanoes cease, and to be awake is
more lovely than dreams

FROM BREATH

POEM 3

Redwood grove, Sinkyone spirit, and sea
rumor of wind between them
throat quivers, hawk keens
restless waves cull your heart.

Rivers lull the ocean in your veins
tides shape my body to your desire.
Hold me until my breath becomes
a delirium of elements between us.

In the distant mist foghorn sobs
an awful silence follows
your shoulders soft as cloud bank
save my mouth from the cut of its screams.

In your eyes twilight resonates
mysterious hue as day turns and expires.
Across forgotten coast, wild grasses
turn to the sea, my lips shape your name
echo the turbulence of our bodies.

Joan Larkin

WANT

She wants an old house full of cups and the ghosts
of last century's lesbians; I want a spotless
apartment, a fast computer. She wants a woodstove,
three cords of ash, an axe; I want
a clean gas flame. She wants a row of jars:
oats, coriander, thick green oil;
I want nothing to store. She wants pomanders,
linens, baby quilts, scrapbooks. She wants Wellesley
reunions. I want gleaming floorboards, the river's
reflection. She wants shrimp and sweat and salt;
she wants chocolate. I want a raku bowl,
steam rising from rice. She wants goats,
chickens, children. Feeding and weeping. I want
wind from the river freshening cleared rooms.
She wants birthdays, theaters, flags, peonies.
I want words like lasers. She wants a mother's
tenderness. Touch ancient as the river.
I want a woman's wit swift as a fox.
Meanwhile, she's in her city, meeting
her deadline; I'm in my mill village out late
with the dog, listening to the pinging wind bells,
        thinking
of the twelve years of wanting, apart and together.
Meanwhile, we've kissed all weekend, we want
to drive the hundred miles and try it again.

DREAM: BAY FOAL

for Roz

I was given a beauty
wide sweet head
and I rubbed her right
between the eyes.
She pressed hard
against my palm. She adored
me. Soft gray eyelids, nostrils
of the same smokey flesh.
Velvet mouth and nose
whiskers.

She curled, all legs, in my lap
her hooves held high
in the air   dark horn
tips   from the rippling basket
of limbs she formed
in my arms: A love.

The muscles in her flanks
liquid as I stroked
and rubbed her down.
Her new bones turned easy
muscles gliding between
my fingers, almost fingers themselves,

the deep pleasure pushing back
the chords of power
under her beautiful brown
skin. This cannot keep
up   I thought   the first cold
to enter the dream.

Full gaze.
She turned her muscled neck
thick shiny chestnut
then nibbled   sucking, pulling
on all my fingers
in twos and threes.

To think I almost gave
the foal away
to play with a braid
of wind and cold
and doubt.

LOVING IN THE WAR YEARS

Loving you is like living
in the war years.
I *do* think of Bogart & Bergman
not clear who's who
but still singin a long smoky
mood into the piano bar
drinks straight up
the last bottle in the house
while bombs split
outside, a broken
world.

A world war going on
but you and I still insisting
in each our own heads
still thinkin how
if I could only make some contact
with that woman across the keyboard
we size each other up
    yes . . .

Loving you has this kind of desperation
to it, like do or die, I
having eyed you from the first
time you made the decision to move

from your stool
to live dangerously.

All on the hunch
that in our exchange of photos
of old girlfriends, names
of cities and memories
back in the states
the fronts we've manned
out here on the continent
all this on the hunch
that *this* time there'll be
no need for resistance.

Loving in the war years
calls for this kind of risking
without a home to call our own
I've got to take you as you come
to me, each time like a stranger
all over again. Not knowing
what deaths you saw today
I've got to take you
as you come, battle bruised
refusing our enemy, fear.

We're all we've got. You and I

maintaining
this war time morality
where being queer
and female is as rude
as we can get.

Joy Harjo

DESIRE

for J.

Say I chew desire and water is an explosion
of sugar wings in my mouth.

Say it tastes of you.

Say I could drown because you left
for the time it takes a blackbird to understand
a pine tree.

Say we enter the pine woods at dawn.

We never slept and the only opium we smoked
was what became of our mingled breath.

Say the stars have never learned
to say good-bye. (One is a jewel
of blue magic in your perfect ear.)

Say all of this is true and more

than there are blackbirds
in a heaven of blackbirds.

PAULA GUNN ALLEN is the daughter of a Laguna Pueblo, Sioux, and Scottish mother and a Lebanese-American father. A major Native American poet, writer, lecturer, and scholar, she has published seven volumes of poetry, a novel, a collection of essays, and two anthologies. Her most recent work is *Grandmothers of Light: A Medicine Woman's Sourcebook* (Beacon Press).

MARY BARNARD (b. 1910), a poet and translator, is the author of *Assault on Mount Helicon: A Literary Memoir* (University of California Press).

MATILDA BETHAM (1776–1852), a poet, diarist, and compiler, was born in Suffolk, England. In addition to her other works, she published *A Biographical Dictionary of Celebrated Women of Every Age and Country* in 1804.

DIONNE BRAND's poetry collection, *No Language Is Neutral* (Coach House Press) was published in 1990. She lives in Ontario.

OLGA BROUMAS's first volume of poetry, *Beginning With O*, won the Yale Series of Younger Poets competition in 1977. Her other books of poetry include *Pastoral Jazz* and *Perpetua* (both published by Copper Canyon Press).

CHRYSTOS (Menominee) works for Native rights and prisoners' rights. Her books include *Not Vanishing* and *In Her I Am* (both published by Press Gang). She is a winner of the Audre Lorde Poetry Competition sponsored by Cleveland State University, which published her newest book, *Fugitive Colors*, in 1995.

CHERYL CLARKE was born in Washington, D.C. She is the author of four books of poetry: *Narratives: poems in the tradition of black women, Living as a Lesbian, Humid Pitch,* and *Experimental Love,* which was nominated for a 1994 Lambda Award.

KAILA MORRIS COMPTON is a writer and photographer from Los Angeles. She is currently completing a Ph.D. in cultural anthropology at Harvard University.

SOR JUANA INÉS DE LA CRUZ (1648/51–1695) was a Mexican nun, intellectual, and eloquent advocate on behalf of women's involvement in the literary and intellectual spheres. She is considered one of the great Hispanic poets of the seventeenth century.

EMILY DICKINSON (1830–1886) was born and lived in Amherst, Massachusetts. Except for seven anonymous verses, her poems, which number 1,775, were unpublished during her lifetime.

JAN FREEMAN is the author of *Hyena* (Cleveland State University Poetry Center) and *Autumn Sequence* (Paris Press). She is a contributing editor to *The American Poetry Review,* and is working on a new collection of poems entitled *Tenderness.*

BEATRIX GATES, the author of *native tongue* and *Shooting at Night,* has poems anthologized in *Gay & Lesbian Poetry in Our Time* (St. Martin's Press) and *queer city.* Her work has appeared in *The Kenyon Review,* and scenes from her libretto, "The Singing Bridge," were performed in New York City in 1993. Her children's book, *Hawksbill Memory,* is forthcoming.

ELSA GIDLOW (1898–1986) wrote the first North American poetry book to celebrate lesbian love, *On a Grey Thread* (1923), as well as the first full-life, explicitly lesbian autobiography ever published anywhere, *ELSA: I Come with My Songs* (1986). She was the founder of Druid Heights, a California-based, Taoist-inspired retreat.

JEWELLE GOMEZ is the author of a novel, *The Gilda Stories,* and a collection of essays entitled *Forty-Three Septembers* (both published by Firebrand Books). She writes and teaches in the Bay Area.

JANICE GOULD, author of *Beneath My Heart* (Firebrand Books), writes, "I am a mixed-blood of Koyangk'auwi Maidu and European descent. I grew up in California but now live in Albuquerque, New Mexico, with my partner of several years and our many cats. I'm completing my doctoral degree in English at the University of New Mexico."

JUDY GRAHN is well known as a leading feminist poet, theorist, and author. Her books include *Another Mother Tongue, The Work of a Common Woman,* and *Blood, Bread, and Roses: How Menstruation Created the World.* She is cofounder of The Institute for Women's Arts, Mysteries, and Sciences, which teaches her ideas.

MARILYN HACKER is the author of nine books, including *Winter Numbers* and *Selected Poems,* both published by

Norton. *Love, Death, and the Changing of the Seasons,* a verse novel, is available in a new edition from Norton. *Going Back to the River* received a Lambda Literary Award in 1991.

JOY HARJO is of the Creek (Muscogee) Tribe. She is associate professor of English at the University of Arizona, a screenwriter, and a player of tenor sax. Her books of poetry include *She Had Some Horses* (Thunder's Mouth) and *In Mad Love and War* (Wesleyan).

ELOISE KLEIN HEALY's most recent collection, *Artemis in Echo Park* (Firebrand Books), was nominated for the Lambda Book Award and was released as a spoken-word recording on CD and audio cassette from New Alliance records. She teaches at Antioch University in Los Angeles.

MELANIE HOPE is an African–North American lesbian whose most immediate ancestors came to the United States from Guyana and Nevis.

IRENA KLEPFISZ is a poet/activist, teacher, and author of *A Few Words in the Mother Tongue: Poems Selected and New* and *Dreams of an Insomniac: Jewish Feminist Essays, Speeches, and Diatribes.* She serves as editorial consultant on Yiddish language and literature for the Jewish feminist magazine *Bridges.*

JOAN LARKIN is the author of two collections of poetry, *Housework* and *A Long Sound.* She coedited the anthologies *Amazon Poetry* and *Lesbian Poetry* with Elly Bulkin, and *Gay & Lesbian Poetry in Our Time* with Carl Morse

(St. Martin's Press). She has also authored *The AIDS Passion Play,* a play in poems.

AUDRE LORDE (1934–1992) published nine volumes of poetry and five works of prose, including *The Black Unicorn, Sister Outsider, The Cancer Journals, A Burst of Light,* and *Our Dead Behind Us.* She was a recipient of the Walt Whitman Citation of Merit (1991) and was named the New York State Poet (1991–1993).

AMY LOWELL (1874–1925), born in Brookline, Massachusetts, was an early leader in the American Imagist movement. She won the Pulitzer Prize for *What's O'Clock* in 1926.

JANE MILLER's recent books are *August Zero,* winner of the Western States Book Award, and *Working Time: Essays on Poetry, Travel, and Culture.* She is the recipient of a Lila Wallace–Reader's Digest Award in Poetry and is on the faculty of the University of Arizona program in creative writing.

HONOR MOORE's collection of poems is *Memoir* (Chicory Blue Press). Her biography of her grandmother, the painter Margarett Sargent, will be published in 1995.

CHERRÍE MORAGA is a poet, playwright, and essayist. Her works include *Loving in the War Years* and *The Last Generation* (both published by South End Press). She was a coeditor and contributor to the groundbreaking collection entitled *This Bridge Called My Back: Writings by Radical Women of Color.*

EILEEN MYLES comes from Boston and has lived in New York City since the mid-seventies. Her last book of poems, *Not Me,* was published by Semiotext(e) in 1991. She's recently published a collection of stories, *Chelsea Girls,* with Black Sparrow Press.

LINDA L. NELSON is a writer and freelance editor whose work has appeared in several anthologies, and in *Poets & Writers Magazine, Out/Look, The Native,* and elsewhere. She is the Director of New Media and Technology for *The Village Voice* and a former editor of the feminist periodical *Trivia: A Journal of Ideas.*

H. EMILIA PAREDES writes, "I learned to love and speak in Perú my seventeenth year. My blood is from the Amazon region of Perú." She was a 1993 recipient of the Astraea Foundation's Lesbian Writers Fund award. She is a psychiatric social worker at the HIV Care Program at the San Francisco City Clinic.

PAT PARKER (1944–1989), born in Houston, Texas, was the first out lesbian-feminist black poet, and among the earliest out voices for the lesbian-feminist movement. She published five volumes of poetry, including *Movement in Black* and *Jonestown and Other Madness* (both available through Firebrand Books).

GERRY GOMEZ PEARLBERG's writings have appeared in *modern words, Global City Review, Calyx, Sister & Brother: Lesbians and Gay Men Write About Their Lives Together,* and elsewhere. A 1993 winner of the Judith's Room Emerging Talent Poetry Competition, she has recently completed her first collection of poems.

MINNIE BRUCE PRATT has most recently published *Crime Against Nature,* chosen as the 1989 Lamont Poetry Selection by the Academy of American Poets, and *Rebellion: Essays 1980–1991.* She lives in Jersey City, New Jersey, and has completed a volume of sex-and-gender-bending prose, *S/he* (Firebrand Books).

ELIZABETH RANDOLPH's writings have appeared in *Color-life Magazine, Cocodrilo,* and *Contemporary Lesbian Writers of the United States: A Bibliographic Critical Sourcebook* (Greenwood Publications). She believes that by the year 2040, love will be available over-the-counter in gelcap or liquid form.

NAOMI REPLANSKY was born in the Bronx, New York, in 1918. Her book *Ring Song* (Scribners, 1952), was nominated for a National Book Award. Her other books include *Twenty-One Poems, Old and New* (Ginkgo Press) and *The Dangerous World* (Another Chicago Press). She lives in New York City.

ADRIENNE RICH has published more than fifteen volumes of poetry, two collections of essays and speeches, and a feminist study of motherhood. Her most recent book, *What Is Found There: Notebooks on Poetry and Politics* (Norton) was published in 1993.

CHRISTINA ROSSETTI (1830–1894), born in London, was the author of six volumes of poetry. Her best known work is *Goblin Market and Other Poems,* published in 1862.

MURIEL RUKEYSER (1913–1980) dropped out of college with the advent of the Depression. Her first book was published at age twenty-one. She was active in the far left in the thirties and, by coincidence, was in Spain on the first day of the civil war there. A single mother, by choice, she lived, as well as wrote, as a pioneering feminist.

SAPPHO, one of the great lyric poets of Greece, is believed to have been born on the Greek island of Eresus around 612 B.C. About a hundred or so of her poems and fragments have survived to the present day.

MAY SARTON, the Belgium-born American poet and novelist, was born in 1912. Her most recent volumes of poetry include *Letters from Maine, The Silence Now: New and Uncollected Poems,* and *Collected Poems 1930–1993.* She lives in Maine.

RUTH L. SCHWARTZ lives in Oakland, California, with her lover and their menagerie. A recipient of fellowships from the NEA and the Astraea Foundation's Lesbian Writers Fund, she has published poetry in numerous journals. She worked as an AIDS educator for eight years.

MAUREEN SEATON is the author of *The Sea Among the Cupboards* (New Rivers) and *Fear of Subways* (Eighth Mountain). She was a 1994 recipient of an NEA fellowship and an Illinois Arts Council grant. She teaches poetry in Chicago.

GERTRUDE STEIN (1874–1946) was an American poet, playwright, novelist, and literary experimentalist. Her works include *Three Lives* (1909), *Tender Buttons* (1914), and *The Autobiography of Alice B. Toklas* (1933).

MAY SWENSON (1919–1989) received numerous honors during her career as a poet, including Guggenheim and Rockefeller fellowships, and an Award in Literature from the National Institute of Arts and Letters. Her books include *In Other Words* (1987) and *The Love Poems of May Swenson* (1991).

ALAN S. TRUEBLOOD, Professor Emeritus of Hispanic studies and comparative literature at Brown University, is the author of *Experience and Artistic Expression in Lope de Vega: The Making of La Dorotea* and translator of *Antonio Machado: Selected Poems* (both Harvard University Press).

TERRY WOLVERTON's collection of poems, *Black Slip* (Clothespin Fever Press), was nominated for a Lambda Book Award. She is the coeditor of *Indivisible: New Short Fiction by West Coast Gay and Lesbian Writers* (Plume) and editor of *Blood Whispers: L.A. Writers on AIDS* (Silverton Books/GLCSC).

Author-Title Index

Index of First Lines